LAUGH-OUT-LOUD JOKES

LAUGH-OUT-LOUD MONSTER JOKES

CAITIE MCANENEY

WINDMILL BOOKS

Published in 2025 by Windmill Books, an Imprint of Rosen Publishing
2544 Clinton St., Buffalo, NY 14224

First Edition

Editor: Caitie McAneney
Book Design: Claire Zimmermann

Photo Credits: Cover, p.1 (child) Cookie Studio/Shutterstock.com; cover, pp. 1, 4, 8, 14, 18, 22 (illustrations) Nadzin/Shutterstock.com; series art (paper texture) OanaGherghe2/Shutterstock.com; p. 5 PeopleImages.com - Yuri A/Shutterstock.com; pp. 6, 16, 20 (hand illustrations) HappyPictures/Shutterstock.com; p. 7 Veronica Louro/Shutterstock.com; p. 9 Inna photographer/Shutterstock.com; p. 10 SofiaV/Shutterstock.com; p. 11 Pressmaster/Shutterstock.com; p. 12 Viktorija Reuta/Shutterstock.com; p. 13 Daria_Art/Shutterstock.com; p. 15 Kuznetsov Dmitriy/Shutterstock.com; p. 17 Ilya Andriyanov/Shutterstock.com; p. 19 Pixel-Shot/Shutterstock.com; p. 21 LightField Studios/Shutterstock.com.

Library of Congress Cataloging-in-Publication Data

Names: McAneney, Caitie, author.
Title: Laugh-out-loud monster jokes / Caitie McAneney.
Description: Buffalo, New York : Windmill Books, 2025. | Series: Laugh-out-loud jokes | Includes index.
Identifiers: LCCN 2024010246 (print) | LCCN 2024010247 (ebook) | ISBN 9781538396926 (library binding) | ISBN 9781538396919 (paperback) | ISBN 9781538396933 (ebook)
Subjects: LCSH: Monsters--Juvenile humor.
Classification: LCC PN6231.M665 M33 2025 (print) | LCC PN6231.M665 (ebook) | DDC 818.602--dc23/eng/20230314
LC record available at https://lccn.loc.gov/2024010246
LC ebook record available at https://lccn.loc.gov/2024010247

Manufactured in the United States of America

CPSIA Compliance Information: Batch #CSWM25. For further information, contact Rosen Publishing at 1-800-237-9932

CONTENTS

Little Monsters 4
Fun with Frankenstein 6
Witches in Stitches 8
Mummy Madness 10
Under the Sea 12
Monster Mash 14
Zombie Zingers 16
Grab a Bite 18
Witty Werewolves 20
Glossary 22
For More Information 23
Index 24

Words in the glossary appear in **bold** the first time they are used in the text.

LITTLE MONSTERS

What do little monsters play?

HIDE AND SHRIEK.

What do little monsters use at the playground?

THE SCARY-GO-ROUND.

What do little monsters eat with their strawberries?

WHIPPED SCREAM.

What's a little monster's favorite snack?

GHOUL SCOUT COOKIES.

FUN FACT!

A ghoul is an evil spirit or **phantom**. **Legend** says that they eat dead bodies.

FUN WITH FRANKENSTEIN

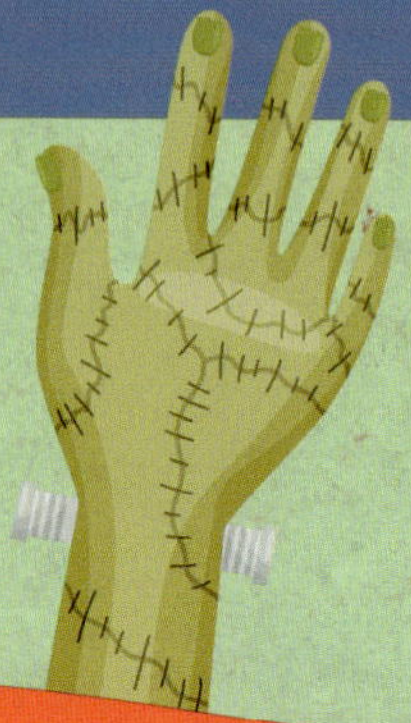

Why did Frankenstein's monster chuckle?

THE DOCTOR HAD HIM IN STITCHES.

What car does Frankenstein drive?

A MONSTER TRUCK.

What do you call a monster in the forest?

FRANKEN-PINE.

Who was the smartest monster to ever live?

FRANK EINSTEIN.

FUN FACT!

Author Mary Shelley wrote Frankenstein (1818) when she was just a teenager.

WITCHES IN STITCHES

What do little witches learn in school?

SPELLING.

Why did the witch leave the party early?

SHE WAS ONLY STOPPING BY FOR A SPELL.

Why can't you tell twin witches apart?

YOU NEVER KNOW WHICH WITCH IS WHICH!

How do you make a witch itch?

GET RID OF THE W!

FUN FACT!

From 1692 to 1693, the Salem witch trials took place in Salem, Massachusetts. More than 200 people were **accused** of witchcraft, and at least 20 died.

MUMMY MADNESS

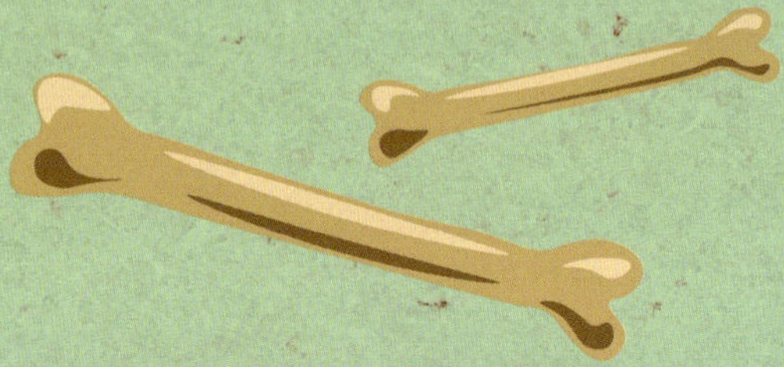

What did the mummy say after filming his movie?

"THAT'S A WRAP!"

What do mummies call their parents?

MUMMY AND DEADY.

Where did the mummy go for his achy bones?

THE CAIRO-PRACTOR.

Do mummies like sandwiches?

NO, THEY PREFER WRAPS.

FUN FACT!

Cairo is the capital of Egypt. **Ancient** Egypt is famous for its mummies.

UNDER THE SEA

Why did the sea monster need lip balm?

HER LIPS WERE KRAKEN.

What did the sea monster say when her friend told a joke?

"STOP—YOU'RE KRAKEN ME UP!"

What did the sea monster eat for dinner?

FISH N' SHIPS.

Which body of water has the most monsters?

THE DEAD SEA.

FUN FACT!

Krakens are huge legendary sea monsters much like giant squids. They're said to have **attacked** ships.

MONSTER MASH

How does a monster style its hair?

IT USES SCARESPRAY!

How do monsters wash their hair?

THEY USE SHAMBOO!

Which monster is the best dancer?

THE BOOGIE MAN.

What's a monster's favorite soup?

SCREAM OF MUSHROOM.

FUN FACT!

The bogeyman is a monster in **folklore** that is often talked about to scare children.

ZOMBIE ZINGERS

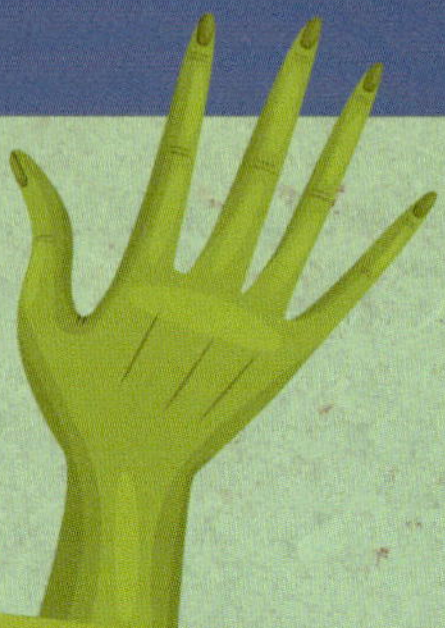

Why did the zombie skip work?

HE FELT ROTTEN.

Why don't zombies go skydiving?

THEY DON'T HAVE THE GUTS.

Why don't zombies eat clown brains?

THEY TASTE FUNNY!

What do zombies call a brain freeze?

FROZEN DINNER.

FUN FACT!

Night of the Living Dead (1968) is one of the most famous zombie movies of all time.

GRAB A BITE

What do you call a vampire who likes to eat chips?

SNACKULA.

Why did the vampire friends go to a cave?

THEY WANTED TO HANG OUT.

How are vampires like **dentures**?

THEY ONLY COME OUT AT NIGHT.

What do you call a vampire doing a cartwheel?

AN ACRO-BAT.

FUN FACT!

Count Dracula was a vampire from the 1897 novel *Dracula* by Bram Stoker. He lived in a castle in Transylvania.

WITTY WEREWOLVES

Which is the hardest monster to find?

A WHERE WOLF.

What did the werewolf read each morning?

HER HORROR-SCOPE.

What happened when the werewolf swallowed a clock?

HE GOT TICKS.

Did you hear about the werewolves at the comedy show?

THEY WERE HOWLING ALL NIGHT!

FUN FACT!

Werewolves have been part of folklore as far back as ancient Greece and Rome.

GLOSSARY

accuse: To blame.

ancient: From a long time ago.

attack: To try to harm someone or something.

dentures: A set of false teeth.

folklore: The stories and ways of a group of people from a certain place or country that are handed down through the years.

howl: The long, loud cry of a wild animal, such as a wolf or dog. Also, to laugh loudly.

legend: A story coming down from the past that is popularly accepted but cannot be checked.

phantom: A ghost or something else that seems real but is not real.

FOR MORE INFORMATION

BOOKS

Clarke, Ginjer. *Are Sea Monsters Real?* New York, NY: Penguin Young Readers, 2022.

Owen, Ruth. *Witches.* Minneapolis, MN: Bearport Publishing Company, 2021.

Yorke, Malcolm. *Beastly Tales.* New York, NY: DK Publishing, 2023.

WEBSITES

Vampire
kids.britannica.com/kids/article/vampire/600681
Learn more about vampires, including their freaky features.

Weird but True!: Halloween
kids.nationalgeographic.com/weird-but-true/article/halloween-1
Explore fun facts about Halloween with National Geographic Kids.

INDEX

Cairo, Egypt, 10, 11

Dead Sea, 12

folklore, 15, 21

Frankenstein, 6, 7

ghouls, 4, 5

Kraken, 12, 13

legends, 5, 13

little monsters, 4

mummies, 10, 11

Night of the Living Dead, 17

Salem, Massachusetts, 9

Shelley, Mary, 7

Transylvania, 19

vampire, 18

werewolves, 20, 21

witches, 9, 10

zombies, 16, 17